DJ

Earning $50,000–$100,000 with a High School Diploma or Less

Announcer

Car Mechanic

Chef

Cosmetologist

DJ

Dog Groomer

Energizing Energy Markets:
Clean Coal, Shale, Oil, Wind, and Solar

Farming, Ranching, and Agriculture

Masseur & Massage Therapist

Personal Assistant

Presenting Yourself: Business Manners,
Personality, and Etiquette

Referee

The Arts: Dance, Music, Theater, and Fine Art

Truck Driver

Earning $50,000–$100,000 with a High School Diploma or Less

DJ

CHRISTIE MARLOWE

MASON CREST

Mason Crest
450 Parkway Drive, Suite D
Broomall, PA 19008
www.masoncrest.com

Printed in the United States of America.

First printing
9 8 7 6 5 4 3 2 1

Series ISBN: 978-1-4222-2886-9
ISBN: 978-1-4222-2892-0
ebook ISBN: 978-1-4222-8928-0

The Library of Congress has cataloged the
        hardcopy format(s) as follows:

            Library of Congress Cataloging-in-Publication Data

Marlowe, Christie.
  DJ / Christie Marlowe.
      pages cm. – (Earning $50,000 - $100,000 with a high school diploma or less)
  Includes bibliographical references and index.
      ISBN 978-1-4222-2892-0 (hardcover) – ISBN 978-1-4222-2886-9 (series) –
ISBN 978-1-4222-8928-0 (ebook)
  1. Disc jockeys–Vocational guidance–Juvenile literature. I. Title.
  ML3795.M178 2014
  781.64023–dc23
                            2013015556

Produced by Vestal Creative Services.
www.vestalcreative.com

Contents

CHAPTER 1

Careers Without College

Who plays the music at a party, a club, or on the radio? Chances are, it is a DJ. A disc jockey is a person who provides music for an audience. Sometimes this audience is a small crowd, while at other times it is a group of people large enough to fill a concert hall. Radio DJs reach the largest audience because their shows are broadcast to anyone within several miles. As long as listeners are within range, they can tune in.

"Being a DJ isn't just a job. It's a lifestyle," Eric Tormen explains. With over twenty years of experience as a mobile and club disc jockey, Eric has a completely different schedule than the average person. "It's a lot of late nights. Whether I'm working at a party or at a club, I

DJ Kool Herc is credited with starting hip-hop music in the early 1970s. He was the first DJ to isolate the instrumental portion of the record, which emphasized the drum beat—the "break"—and switch from one break to another. This breakbeat DJing, using hard funk, rock, and records with Latin-music beats, formed the basis of hip-hop music. Kool Herc's DJ style was then adopted by other great DJs such as Afrika Bambaataa and Grandmaster Flash.

The History of DJs

For much of the twentieth century, all music was stored on records—vinyl discs with grooves in them "read" by a needle. The earliest DJs switched between songs by changing records on their turntables. A truly talented DJ might even "scratch," or push a record underneath the needle to make a scratching noise as the audio on the record was forced to play very fast. If this was done in rhythm with the music, it made a sound that people liked.

Eventually, compact discs (CDs) were developed, and DJs used these instead. Today, almost all music is stored electronically on a computer. A DJ will still use a turntable to control the music, but this turntable acts more like a controller than a player. However, vinyl records are becoming more popular again today, and most artists release their music on records as well as CDs. Thanks to how much technology has advanced, a DJ has more options today to choose from.

usually don't get home until well after midnight. Even after an event is over, I need to pack up all my equipment and drive home, which can take a long time." Radio DJs can also have odd hours. "Do you ever listen to the radio while you are waking up in the morning?" Eric asks. "What you might not realize is that a radio DJ is providing that music for you and has probably already been at the station for a few hours."

Being a DJ requires a lot of time and dedication. You can't become successful overnight, but if you work very hard, it can pay off. Because you don't need a college degree, you must be able to prove how good you are based on your skill alone. "The real challenge is showing that you are better than the average DJ," Eric insists. "You need to make a name

A DJ needs a certain kind of personality. He can't be shy!

for yourself if you really want to go somewhere. If people like what they hear, you are more likely to be recommended and called again." In the world of entertainment, this is known as networking.

In addition to the technical skill required, DJs must also feel comfortable with talking to a lot of different people. "Being shy is not an option," Eric warns. "No matter what, you're going to have to interact with people." Radio DJs will take calls and perform interviews on air. Party DJs might also act as an MC, or master of ceremonies. The MC speaks with the crowd and encourages them to get out on the dance floor. In many cases, the MC is the "life of the party." Even if a concert DJ doesn't speak to the audience, he or she must still perform for a lot of different people. Just like a musician, a DJ must know how to deal with stage fright.

A Changing Industry

As an entertainer, a DJ relies completely on music, and music is constantly changing. A song that is popular this week might not be remembered in a few years. When asked how many songs a DJ needs to have, Eric Tormen says, "I have thousands of songs on my computer. Some are decades old and others just came out yesterday. You never know what song people will want to hear, and a good DJ is always ready for anything. Telling someone I don't have a song is unacceptable."

Updating his music collection isn't the only thing Eric needs to worry about. "Every day, other DJs are coming up with new techniques on how they play music. Sometimes it's hard to keep up. Just switching from one song to another is never enough. If people wanted to just listen to music, they could do that at home. DJs are expected to give a performance."

A nightclub DJ often "performs" as well as plays music.

The most talented live DJs "mix" music on the spot. This involves interacting two completely different songs while playing them. For example, a DJ might use the background music from one song and the vocals from another one. "An audience enjoys when a DJ mixes music because the music is completely unique," Eric explains. "It is something that has only been played there, and will never be played quite the same way again." In this way, a DJ is also partially a musician and producer. A DJ might even take it a step further by adding in "samples" of an additional song. Samples are usually very short audio clips and might consist of a short word or a catchy sound.

Mixing and using samples are just two examples of how technology has improved a DJ's ability to perform. As technology advances, a whole array of new tools will be out there to consider. This might seem discouraging, but Eric sees it in a positive light. "Each year, new equipment is coming out, and with it, new possibilities. Even after twenty years, I'm still learning something new. I couldn't ever get bored of being a DJ."

The College Question

Eric Tormen always knew he wanted to be a DJ. He loved playing music, but he wasn't interested in writing or performing it himself like a musician would. Instead, he wanted to take the music that already existed and make other people happy with it. Becoming a DJ just seemed like the best choice for him. Because the job requires so much technical skill, Eric Tormen was surprised when he found out he wouldn't need to go to college to be successful. "I quickly learned that there was no true college degree for a DJ," he says. "Anything I was going to learn, I would need to learn on my own."

In an industry where the technology is developing at the same time that people's tastes are constantly changing, a DJ has to be willing to be flexible and learn new skills.

In a way, Eric was relieved. College can be expensive and take up to four years to complete. Many graduating students are thousands of dollars in debt by the time they earn their degree. "While so many of my friends went away to college, I was already getting into the business of being a DJ. It was hard at first, but by the time they graduated, I was already making great money. Plus, I wasn't in debt like my friends were. I didn't owe anyone money."

Because he wasn't going to college, Eric had a lot of free time to perfect his skills, but it wasn't easy. All the money for the equipment he needed to buy had to come from somewhere. "I had to work at plenty of odd jobs before I was ready to pursue my dream job. I spent time working at a clothing store, a gas station, and a supermarket. I needed the money to support myself while I tried to make it as a DJ."

In the end, Eric's hard work was worth it. In just a few short years, Eric Tormen was able to make enough money as a DJ to leave his other jobs behind. The freedom of learning at his own pace also came with its own set of challenges, however. "At first, I didn't know what I was doing. There were no books to read or classes I could go to. I ended up asking my friends and other DJs for advice. Today, others ask me for advice on how to become a DJ—and I am more than happy to give it."

Learning Outside the Classroom

Like all DJs, Eric started out with the basics. He learned how to switch between two songs smoothly. Learning how to use a DJ's equipment can be very overwhelming at first. Other skills than just technical ones are required as well. For example, a good DJ knows how to "read" a crowd—in other words, she understands what people want to hear.

A party DJ must be responsive to the crowd's mood.

The ability to sense whether upbeat dance music or slow-dance music is a better match for the crowd's mood is very important to a DJ's success. Eric adds, "If a DJ pleases the crowd, he or she will probably be hired again. But this is

one of those skills that only comes with experience. No one can teach it to you."

After learning as much as he could, Eric was ready to test out his skills at small parties. Just because he was playing for a small crowd didn't mean he wasn't nervous, though! "There were only about thirty people at my first party, but I was so scared," he remembers. "I messed up really bad a few times, but no one seemed to notice because they were all having such a great time. After my first few gigs, I got a lot better, and I wasn't as anxious."

Starting out as a DJ today is much different than what it was like when Eric first began. "DJs today might have it easier than I did," Eric explains. "In my day, all I could do was ask others for advice. I relied on whatever I could learn from more experienced DJs or could figure out for myself. Today, aspiring DJs can look up almost anything online."

What Eric says has some truth to it. While you should still learn all you can from successful DJs, some of what you learn can be found online. The Internet is an invaluable resource for an up-and-coming DJ! Today, there are even lessons an **aspiring** DJ can sign up for and attend online.

"I'm not going to lie. Sometimes it gets tiring," Eric admits. "It's a tough job, but I wouldn't trade it for the world. Nothing beats the rush of watching people enjoy the music you are playing for them."

CHAPTER 2

What Do DJs Do?

When you think of a DJ, what do you imagine? One person might think about an announcer in front of a microphone conducting interviews at a radio station. Another person might be reminded of a big concert hall with a performer mixing music live on stage. Some people will think back to the last party they were at, where a DJ played loud music and encouraged guests to dance. A DJ's job is as **diverse** as the role a DJ needs to fill, which makes all these interpretations correct!

Looking at the Words

Something that is **diverse** has lots of variety—many different kinds of things—included in it.

Expertise is skill in a particular area.

A DJ's biggest job is as an entertainer playing music for a crowd. Where you choose to perform, however, is completely up to you. There are three main categories of disc jockeys: radio DJs, concert DJs, and mobile DJs. As a DJ with almost twenty-five years of experience, Alexia Karner has performed in all three areas. "I started out as a radio DJ," she says. "I thought that's all I wanted to do, but when I was offered a job as a mobile DJ a few years later, I decided to give it a try."

Alexia's experience is not at all uncommon. Many DJs choose to work in more than one area for all sorts of reasons. In Alexia's case, it was a mixture of pay and curiosity. "I was able to make a lot more money by working two jobs, but I had so much fun between being a radio DJ and a mobile DJ that it didn't really feel like I was working."

Different kinds of DJs share some common equipment and knowledge. All DJs, for example, know how to use audio equipment. Their level of **expertise** depends on what they are doing, but even a radio DJ must know how to switch between songs and adjust the volume.

Even though DJs must have a lot of technical knowledge, they do not need a college degree, and the reason behind this is simple. "Not much of what a DJ does can be learned in school," Alexia explains. "Sure you can take some lessons, but mostly it's just something you learn over time. The more experienced you are, the better you will be. As long as you can perform, it doesn't matter if you went to college."

Picking a Name

Like musicians, DJs often pick a special name to be known as while they are performing. Some DJs choose to pick a variation of their real name. For instance, a person named Chris John might choose to take the name DJ KrisJon. Another DJ might make a name based off of his or her initials. Alexia Karner became DJ AKay. Some DJs pick a name based off a childhood nickname or one of their specific interests. No matter what name you pick, be careful not to choose the same name as a DJ that already exists.

Radio DJs

Some of the most famous DJs are also radio announcers. Since many people listen to the radio while waking up or driving, a radio DJ can become a household name. A radio DJ can spend most of his or her time picking music to be played for thousands of people to hear. Being a radio DJ is much more than playing music, however.

A radio DJ is as much an announcer as a performer. Alexia Karner is often told what stories she needs to cover, even if she is given the freedom to decide how to speak about it. When asked about what a typical day at the radio station was like, Alexia says, "I usually spend time talking about a little bit of everything from the news, weather, traffic, you name it! I need to talk about anything people would want to hear about

A DJ must be able to keep track of many things at once: turntables, mixers, microphones . . . and most important, his audience.

on the radio. Sometimes I am even asked to read commercials." Commercials are just one way a radio station makes its money.

For the people who rely on the radio for much of their news, the job is very exciting. "Because we don't need actual video footage like a television news channel, radio stations are sometimes the first to report a new story. I love it when listeners call in to comment on our news stories. I get to meet a lot of people even when I'm sitting at the radio station." A radio station is always running, which means a radio DJ can have very irregular hours. "When I first started working for this radio station, I was given the overnight shift. I worked from midnight until six am." Fortunately, Alexia was able to ask for a better shift as she became more respected as a radio DJ.

When asked what she liked most about being a radio DJ, Alexia says, "One of my favorite parts of the job is performing interviews. I get to work with so many different people throughout the day." Preparing for an interview is very hard work, though. Alexia must think up questions and be ready to ask follow-up questions on the spot. In order to know what to ask, she must perform a lot of research beforehand.

Another way Alexia gets to meet people is by hosting a lot of events outside of the station. Larger radio stations might hold contests, competitions, or even visit large music events. "I can't even tell you how many musicians I've met over the years," Alexia recalls. "It's one thing to play their music at the station, but it's another to speak with them face to face. That's pretty cool!"

Working at a radio station can restrict you quite a bit, though. Many radio stations specialize in one type of music, such as Rock or Pop. If you want to DJ a particular kind of music, apply to a radio station that plays the type of music you would like to play. Each week, a list of the forty most popular songs in a musical **genre** is released, known as the "top-forty" chart. Because these songs are the most popular, they will be played most often on a radio station. Alexia Karner warns, "As a radio DJ, you will hear the most popular songs many times before they are removed from the top-forty chart." A song can remain on the top-forty lists for weeks or even months. "Even after they are removed," Alexia continues, "they will probably be played every once in a while. In order

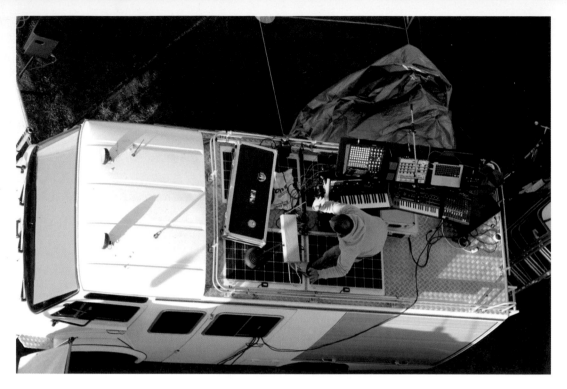

Sometimes both radio DJs and party DJs take it on the road—literally. This DJ is working at an outdoor festival from on top his van.

to enjoy the job, you must be okay with this. Otherwise, you can get pretty sick of hearing the same songs over and over. You don't get to mix it up, just because you want to hear something new!"

In addition to understanding and playing music, a radio DJ must have plenty of additional skills. For example, being an announcer means you must have a clear, strong voice. You also have to be able to keep your cool under pressure. Alexia says, "It isn't always easy to speak on the spot. You can't get nervous when you're on air. Some of what an interviewee or a caller tells you might be surprising, but you have to remain as calm and as natural as possible. It won't be easy at first, but it will get better with time." She also says that being a radio DJ requires time-management skills. "I need to know how much music to fit in during an hour, how many commercials I need to read, and when I will have time to perform interviews. All of this must be planned long before my show starts. I can't rush anything, and I can't just wing

it as I go along." Still, she wouldn't have it any other way. "Being a radio DJ is very rewarding, which is why I've chosen to stay here so long."

Looking at the Words

When someone is **commissioned**, she's been hired to do a specific job.

Mobile DJs

While working at the radio station, Alexia Karner went to work at the same place pretty much every day, unless she was doing a special event. However, not every DJ stays in one place that way. Mobile DJs are required to travel quite a bit to perform at different events. Unlike radio DJs, mobile DJs do not work for just one person or company. They are usually **commissioned** to provide entertainment for weddings, parties, or private business events.

A mobile DJ's technical knowledge might need to be better than a radio disc jockey's. In addition to knowing how to run the equipment, a mobile DJ must also know how it works. Alexia explains, "If something goes wrong with my equipment while I'm at an event, it's up to me to fix it. I can't just call someone else to do it. If I can't fix the problem, I won't be able to perform. That's a lot of pressure!" In addition to a DJ controller and computer, a mobile DJ might also bring lights and speakers to the show. "At these events," Alexia says, "a mobile DJ truly becomes a one-person entertainment crew."

The DJ at a wedding reception may have extra duties besides playing music. She's often the one who organizes and narrates the various significant moments of the reception, such as the moment when the newly-wed couple cuts the cake.

Sometimes, an MC, or master of ceremonies, is hired in addition to a DJ. An additional person is more expensive, though, and some clients prefer to leave all the work up to a DJ. "When this happens," Alexia says, "a mobile DJ could also be put in charge of the special events at a party." During a wedding, for example, a DJ might lead the cake-cutting ceremony or the moment when the bride throws the bouquet. Without an MC, the DJ becomes one of the only experts of audio equipment. When the bride and groom's family wish to speak, the mobile DJ might be asked to provide a microphone.

Although it might seem easy to run a party, there can be a lot to remember! "There is a special order to events at a party, and a mobile DJ needs to keep track of all of them. If a party is six hours long, a DJ needs to figure out how to space everything out evenly while also keeping the guests entertained with music." For example, when should the DJ plan to have the cake cut at a wedding reception? It will need to be after the guests are fed. After all, dessert cannot be served before people eat dinner. "I usually need to communicate with the other people working at the party," Alexia says, "such as the caterers, to ensure everything goes smoothly. A lot more goes into a private event than guests might realize."

Like any entertainer, being a mobile DJ requires preparation. What type of music would the guests like to hear? Mobile DJs are likely one of the most restricted DJs in terms of the music they can play. Parties require an assortment of music, but often from a single genre. They usually must cater to whatever the people hiring the DJ want to hear.

Many of the people who hire mobile DJs will give a specific list of music they want played, as well as music that should never be played. A "do-not-play list" is very common for mobile DJ events. For a wedding, a bride and groom will pick a certain song to be played during their first dance. Even the little things can be a very big deal. Alexia says, "The first-dance song is very significant between a newlywed couple,

A club DJ must be responsive to the club's clientele—and she must be willing to work late nights.

and may not be a very common song. If I don't make sure I have that song before I arrive, it could ruin a very special moment."

To Alexia, the pressure of being a mobile DJ is worth it. "It's very different from being a radio DJ. I'm playing for a much smaller audience, and I get the satisfaction of knowing I have helped create a special day that the guests will never forget."

Concert and Club DJs

Later in her career, Alexia Karner was hired to perform at concerts. Concert DJs are considered some of the most talented DJs because they create music live on stage for a large audience. In this way, a concert DJ is like a musician. "I have to constantly think up new ideas," Alexia says. "I can't play the same song twice. I have to find new ways to mix different songs together and make it sound new."

Another type of concert DJ might play in a club or a bar. A club or bar will have a much smaller crowd and also has other restrictions. For instance, a club might only want you to play a certain type of music. "If you choose to work in a club or a bar, be prepared for some pretty late nights," Alexia advises. "The weekend parties don't usually end until three of four in the morning, and I'm lucky if I get home before the sun comes up."

In addition to performing, concert DJs might also be producing their own music offstage. "Some concert DJs make their own music and then recreate it live in a concert hall. Others take songs that someone else wrote and find a new way of playing them. As far as I see it, as long as people are entertained," Alexia concludes, "a concert DJ is doing a good job."

Concert DJs are usually paid very well. The best concert DJs might even be flown all over the world in order to perform in different countries!

CHAPTER 3

How Can I Become a DJ?

Although there are many different types of disc jockeys, there are only a few ways to become successful as a DJ. The most important trait a DJ must have is **persistence**! Everyone starts from somewhere, and even the most

Looking at the Words

Persistence is the ability to keep going without giving up.

A DJ must be willing to work nights and weekends. The job can be a lot of fun—but it can also mean sometimes missing out on a normal social life with your friends.

experienced DJ was a beginner at some point. Before attempting to get started, an aspiring DJ may spend months observing those who are already successful in the field. Next time you attend a catered party, a concert, or listen to the radio, pay special attention to how a DJ speaks or acts. These people are a great example for young DJs because they have already learned what it takes to do well in the industry.

At only twenty-six years old, Chris John has recently become successful as a mobile DJ. "It was a long road, but I never thought about giving up, and I'm glad that I didn't. I know I still have a long way to go."

DJs fill many different roles, and will always be needed. In fact, radio DJs alone account for over 50,000 jobs in the United States!

Is DJing Right for Me?

Working as a DJ can lead to a very fulfilling career, but before you go out and buy your first set of speakers, consider the many trials a typical DJ must face. "There are so many changes to get used to," Chris begins. "Being a DJ is not your typical nine-to-five job. I didn't realize how much my sleep schedule would change until I became a DJ." Chris works during the evening, and he usually doesn't arrive home until early in the morning. This might not bother night owls, but for someone who prefers waking up early in the morning, this can be a big concern.

A DJ's schedule is different from other occupations' in another way. Many parties and events happen during the weekend, which means a DJ might work during the weekends and rest during the week. Even radio DJs must endure a difficult schedule. Because a radio station is running at all hours of the day, a radio DJ might be up all night. A more experienced radio DJ may be given better hours.

"At first, it really bummed me out," Chris recalls. "I couldn't go out with my friends because I was always working." Once Chris became successful, he had more freedom, and he could choose which nights he wanted to work.

The job has social demands, too. "Being a DJ really forced me to come out of my shell," Chris says. "I used to be terrified of talking to strangers, but now I have no trouble at all." Just because a person is shy, though, doesn't mean he or she wouldn't make a good DJ. Shyness can be overcome! All DJs, though, learn through experience that speaking with people while on the job is absolutely necessary. Chris assures aspiring DJs, "The hardest part was taking that first leap. The rest seemed to come naturally."

Taking Requests

When you call into a radio station and ask the DJ to play a song you want to hear, you are making a request. With the exception of concert DJs, almost every other type of DJ are often asked to play requests. Choosing to play a requested song has its advantages and disadvantages. By playing a request, you might be more liked by your audience. However, it also means you will have to play songs you don't necessarily like. Songs that are popular at the current moment might be requested so much that you are sick of hearing them! But your job is to make your audience happy.

Talent and **enthusiasm** alone will not make you a successful DJ, though. It can take several months or more before you are noticed, but there are ways to increase your chances at success. "You need to learn how to network," Chris advises. "Meet people and prove to them you are a great DJ, even if you are just a beginner. Remember, the best DJs did not become famous overnight." One way of getting yourself out there is by making a CD of your work. "Make hundreds of CDs and give them away or sell them at every event you work at," Chris suggests. "The more people you know, the higher your chances of becoming successful will be." Patience is another key trait any aspiring DJ must have!

Becoming a DJ has many challenges—but many rewards as well. "The job isn't for everyone," Chris John admits, "but for the people who truly want to be a DJ, it is the only job imaginable."

What All DJs Need

Although all DJs play music, this isn't the only requirement for performing the job well. There are a several skills that make for a successful DJ. One of the most important is technical knowledge, understanding how to use **audio** equipment. A radio DJ, for example, often fills the role of an announcer, which requires a set of skills. The Bureau of Labor Statistics lists several important qualities that every announcer should have. The most important for a radio DJ are listed below.

In today's DJ world, computers are a necessity.

- **Computer skills.** Radio DJs should have good computer skills and be able to use computers, editing equipment, and other broadcast-related devices.
- **People skills.** Radio DJs may interview guests and answer phone calls on air. Party DJs and MCs work with clients to plan entertainment options.
- **Persistence.** Entry into this occupation is very competitive, and many auditions may be needed for an opportunity to work on the

air. Many entry-level radio DJs must work for a small station and be flexible to move to a small market to secure their first job. If you're not persistent, chances are you'll give up before you find success in this field.

- **Research skills.** Radio DJs must research the important topics of the day in order to be knowledgeable enough to comment on them during their program.
- **Speaking skills.** Radio DJs must have a pleasant and well-controlled voice, good timing, and excellent pronunciation. Mobile and concert DJs are more like performers than announcers. Along with this new role comes a whole new set of necessary skills. The Bureau of Labor Statistics suggests many important qualities for performers. The skills listed below are based on these suggestions.
- **Discipline.** Talent is not enough for most DJs to find employment in this field. They must constantly practice and seek to improve their technique and style.
- **Physical stamina.** DJs who play in concerts or in nightclubs and those who tour must be able to endure frequent travel and irregular performance schedules.
- **Perseverance.** Finding a job as a DJ can be a frustrating process because it may take a long time. DJs need determination and perseverance to keep trying after receiving many rejections.

Becoming a DJ

"Everyone's journey to becoming a DJ is different," Chris says, "but the most important thing to remember is to have fun while you are doing it." After graduating from high school, Chris spent some time at clubs. "I watched the other DJs on stage and thought about how cool it would

A DJ's most basic equipment: turntables.

be if I could do what they do for a living." Chris John decided to pursue his dream.

"I started out small. I bought some cheap speakers and a used turntable with the money I had saved up over the years. I couldn't afford to buy more music, so I practiced using the music I already owned on my computer."

To someone who has never used a DJ's equipment before, it can seem very confusing, which is why it is important to practice a lot! In time, you will get better. "At first, it felt like learning was a full-time job," says Chris John. "I spent several weeks playing with my new equipment for hours each day. As I got better, my confidence grew."

The main piece of equipment a DJ uses is a turntable, which is made up of two spinning discs and many switches. Each spinning disc controls one track, or song. The switches can be used to adjust the volume or fade between two songs. Because most music is **digital** now, a turntable doesn't always play actual discs. A digital turntable acts as a controller that connects to your computer. When you move the discs with your hands, it changes the speed or position of the song.

"After I perfected how to switch between songs, I started experimenting with all different types of music. My favorite genre is hip hop, but I knew that a good DJ needs to know how to play everything." After becoming comfortable using the equipment, Chris began looking for a job. "I quickly learned that in the entertainment **industry**, networking is everything," Chris recalls. "I didn't know anyone yet, so I knew I needed to find a promoter." Promoters help performers find gigs in exchange for a percentage of what the performer earns from that gig. For example, a promoter might take 25 percent of a DJ's total earnings for a night.

When asked about pay, Chris John says, "After a year of practice, I found an entertainment company that paid me $200 a night to start. I performed three nights a week, and made $600 a week. I was pretty excited. I make a lot more money now, but as a starting salary, it wasn't

> ## Looking at the Words
>
> **Digital** refers to anything that has to do with computer technology.
>
> When people talk about a kind of **industry** like the "music industry" or the "entertainment industry," they're referring to all the activities that go into that particular way of making money.

This DJ is using his headphones to help him "beat match."

bad." Not bad at all, since that's over $30,000 a year without any college experience whatsoever! Because he was only working three nights a week, Chris had the rest of the week to earn money in other ways.

As a DJ becomes more experienced and popular, he or she might decide against using a promoter. Without the need for a promoter, a DJ can make a lot more money. Chris also had more freedom to choose where he wants to work and when. "When I am hired directly by a client, we both save money," he says. Today, Chris John is so popular that he books all his own gigs. As a DJ in high demand, he makes a lot of money doing it!

Headphones

Have you ever seen a DJ leaning into a pair of big headphones with only one ear? Using specialized headphones is one of the ways a DJ is able to plan what the next song will be. Although you cannot hear it, two songs are actually playing on the turntable at once. One of these songs is being played through the speakers while the other is being played through the headphones. A DJ can line up the rhythm of the two songs using the headphones before actually bringing the second song in for the audience to hear. When this tactic is used, it will seem like the first song was meant to continue straight into the second one. Some people may not even notice when the transition happens! "Beat matching" is just one recent advancement in the world of DJs.

CHAPTER 4

How Much
Can I Make?

"When I first decided to become a DJ," Terry Yorn begins, "I wasn't thinking about the money. I had never heard of DJs making more than $100,000 a year, but now I am doing just that." As an extremely successful concert DJ, Terry makes much more than the average DJ's salary. However, he didn't always make this much. "I started out as a radio and mobile DJ making an average salary."

Like many professions, there is a wide range of

Grammy-winning DJ Dubfire says what he likes best about his job is "listening to the crowd and figuring out where to steer them." The crowd at this Dubfire concert clearly likes what he's doing!

pay. As a DJ with so much experience, Terry Yorn has seen how much and how little a DJ can make. According to Terry, "The best way to increase your chances at success are to practice a lot, keep learning, be persistent, and meet a lot of people. If you are talented and **dedicated**, someone will

Looking at the Words

If someone is **dedicated**, she is completely committed and devoted to something; she gives it everything she's got.

eventually take notice." After just fifteen years in the industry, Terry is an example of an extremely successful DJ.

High-Level Earnings

There are plenty of DJs that one day want to make a career out of their passion for music. However, only a few DJs will make it to the top and become very popular. A popular DJ is in higher demand and will usually be paid better for what he or she can do. "I started making more money when I was a mobile DJ," Terry recalls. "I started out making $175 a night, but after a few years in the industry, I was making more than $500 a night." While Terry received a significant raise, though, other DJs continued to be paid at the same rate.

A mobile DJ who makes $500 a night and works three nights a week will make over $70,000 dollars a year! Before Terry Yorn became a concert DJ, he was making as much as $700 a night to play at exclusive clubs and parties. "I couldn't believe how much I was being paid just to do something I love, but I know I am one of the lucky few." Not all mobile DJs will become as popular as Terry did.

Unlike a club or concert DJ, a radio DJ can't interact directly with his audience. The amount of money he makes will depend on the size of the radio station where he works.

"Being paid well as a mobile DJ was great, but the **perks** of being a concert DJ were even better." Once Terry Yorn became a concert DJ, he was asked to play at many different venues. "It was simple at first," he says. "I played within a few hours of where I lived for just a few hundred people. Soon enough, though, I was asked to travel all over the United States. I was flown from state to state just to play concerts. In some ways, it felt like a vacation."

All the expenses of travel were paid for, but the high salary of a concert DJ also comes with a price. Terry Yorn did not have the freedom to choose when or where he would travel. As his popularity grew, he was even asked to perform in

different countries. "I didn't want to leave my friends and family behind, but who could turn down a gig that pays $10,000 a night?" In the end, Terry thinks it is most important to have a balance between family, friends, and work. "I usually travel for a few months and then spend some time at home." With Terry's salary of over $100,000, he can afford to take this kind of time to himself. Like popular musicians, some concert DJs will make millions of dollars, but this is extremely rare.

When it comes to radio DJs, the most well-paid ones work for the most popular stations. Many of these stations are broadcast online for thousands or even millions to hear. A popular radio DJ may also be asked to host special events or interview important celebrities.

Average Salaries

Not every DJ will make the same amount of money as Terry Yorn, but the salary of the average DJ is nothing to complain about. Terry says, "The general rule of thumb is: the larger the audience you reach, the more money you will make." A concert DJ like Terry who plays for thousands of people at a time will make more money than a club DJ who only plays for a hundred.

The average salary for a radio announcer and DJ is about $27,000 per year. However, there is plenty of room to grow within the industry. "Radio DJs who work for a smaller station will make less money, while a DJ who works for a larger, more popular station will make more," Terry explains. "If you want to make a lot of money, you need to aim for the more popular stations."

Most radio stations are small and cannot afford to pay much, which explains the low average. However, technology is drastically changing this trend. Many radio stations are now available through the Internet, which means listeners are not restricted to just the immediate area surrounding a radio station. A listener could be on the other side of the world. This could cause a decline in the numbers of smaller radio stations. "Radio stations will always exist," Terry believes, "but it will be the larger ones that thrive."

Many starting radio DJs work part time, or less than forty hours a week, which causes the average salary to be considerably lower. A full-time radio DJ can expect to make much more than just $27,000 a year. At an average hourly rate of $19.43, a full time radio announcer and DJ could make about $40,000 a year.

Mobile and concert DJs are paid differently. Unlike radio DJs, these DJs are not usually paid using a salary or hourly rate. Instead, they are paid a flat rate based on their performances. How long these nights are and how many nights a DJ can perform are entirely up to the DJ and the people who hire the DJ. Usually, the schedule and pay is agreed upon using a legal document known as a contract. A club DJ might have steady work certain nights a week, but a mobile DJ will need to continually find new events where she can perform.

A mobile DJ can make anywhere between $100 to $500 a night, depending on experience and demand. A popular DJ is much more likely to make $500 per night, while a starting DJ will probably make between $100 and $200. A talented DJ who works for $250 a night three nights per week will make about $39,000 a year. A starting DJ making $100 a night will need to work a lot more often to make even close to that amount of money.

Working only three nights a week might sound appealing, but there is more work that must be done besides the performance itself. "When I wasn't performing, I was trying to find gigs to perform at," Terry says. "I had to meet with each client several times to make sure I knew everything about their special day. Clients don't always know what they want, so another part of my job was advising them—talking to them about their options, helping them make up their minds." When you consider how long it can take to book events and prepare for them, being a mobile DJ could be considered a full-time job!

Radio Stations

Because of the way information was sent out prior to the Internet, radio stations' broadcast area used to be restricted to a circle around their geographical location. One radio station might have only been available in New York City, for example, while another was only available in Seattle. Radio stations could only broadcast using invisible electromagnetic waves that travel through the air. (Other types of electromagnetic waves include microwaves and infrared radiation.) The waves sent out by a radio tower are known radio waves. An antenna on top of a car or stereo is designed to pick up these radio waves. As radio waves are picked up, they are translated into the sounds we can hear. Today, many radio stations are available through the Internet, which does not depend on electromagnetic waves.

CHAPTER 5

Looking to the Future

As entertainers, DJs will always be needed. However, the way people obtain their entertainment is constantly changing. Radio DJs, for example, are not as common as they used to be. While the average growth rate of all occupations within the United States is 14 percent, radio announcers and DJs are only growing between a rate of 5 and 7 percent. Although this is technically still growth, it is far below average.

"There are a few reasons for the low growth rate," Brianna Lonnie

DJs use turntables like this. Nowadays they don't play vinyl discs the way old turntables did.

explains. "One of the biggest reasons is the way technology is changing radio stations."

Brianna Lonnie is a radio DJ and part-time mobile DJ with over forty years in the field. As a result, she has seen how technology has affected all kinds of DJs. Because most radio stations can now be heard on the Internet, there is less need for radio towers or smaller stations. On the other hand, mobile, concert, and club DJs are experiencing about an average rate of growth. Much of their performances are done in person. Unlike the radio, the Internet will not have a direct effect on these positions. However, technology has and will continue to change all DJs over time.

Technology and Advancement

Just ten years ago, most music was on CDs. Before that, tape cassettes were used, and before that, records were the main way to record music. Today, almost all music can be purchased and downloaded digitally. Digital storage has truly changed the way a DJ can perform. For example, it is very easy to change songs on a computer or mp3 player. All you need to do is select the new song and click "play."

One of the most important pieces of equipment a DJ uses is a turntable. These turntables have always been used to play physical discs. Now that music is often all digital, a turntable is more like a controller. The large rotating disc is still there, but the music is on the computer. As the disc spins, the music plays. If a DJ stops the disc, the music will stop. If a

A mixer allows DJs to mix and fade the sound between two turn-tables, while also directing the sound to headphones.

DJ moves the disc forward, the song will move forward at a faster pace, or "fast-forward." In addition to discs, a controller may also have several switches that are used to manipulate the volume, speed, or quality of the sound.

"DJ equipment and software are always evolving," Brianna explains. A computer program is one example of software. "There are several programs that help a DJ perform. As these programs improve, so do the possibilities for a DJ." As an example, some of the newer software programs will find the **tempo** of a song for you. Older versions will require you to figure it out yourself. A DJ who is just starting out might know the basics, but an expert will take it upon him or herself to learn all the tricks of the trade.

"There is a lot more to know about being a DJ than when the field first began," Brianna continues. "The truly talented DJs will do well, but other DJs might not be able to keep up." As the digital age moves forward, this will be more and more true. "If I had any advice for the DJs of the future," Brianna says, "I would tell them: start early, make sure to upgrade your equipment, and keep learning." The technology involved in being a DJ will continue to change, and the most successful DJ will be willing to change with it.

On the flip side, technological advances have also helped radio DJs. Now that radio shows can be pre-recorded, a radio DJ is less likely to work odd hours. Of course, there are always exceptions to this rule. Some radio stations still prefer to hire radio DJs who are willing to work around the clock.

Looking to the Future   **55**

The equipment DJs use is increasingly complicated. DJs need to be comfortable with new technology.

Do You Have a Passion?

There's a lot of talk about passion these days: "Find your passion... Pursue your passion... Do what you love..." But passion, it turns out, lives in all sorts of places. There is only one real formula: try things. Try things and see how they fit. Try jobs and find out what you like—and just as important, find out what you don't like. Passion can come later. Right now, just find something you enjoy. That's a starting point. Maybe it'll become that thing you can do for hours and it feels like only a few minutes have gone by. But don't put that pressure on yourself. Start small.

Adapted from the essay "The Truth About Finding Your Passion" by Colin Ryan. More of his work can be found at his website: http://astanduplife.com.

Conclusion

DJs are a very diverse group, even if they all share a few common characteristics. The people interviewed in this book are very dedicated to what they do, and their stories of success prove it. "Being a DJ is a lot of hard work, but I don't know a single DJ who regrets it," Brianna says.

For many people, going to college is the right decision. In addition to the major you choose to study, you also learn a lot of useful information about life. Unfortunately, not every teenager knows what she wants to do for the rest of her life, and she may not feel ready to pick a lifelong career at such a young age.

You don't need a college degree to be a radio DJ—but you do need plenty of specialized skills.

"I thought about college," Brianna admits. "A degree in journalism might have helped me as an announcer, but I didn't know I wanted to be an announcer at the time." Brianna chose not to go to college because she wasn't sure what she wanted to study. Many students encounter this same problem. "After some time, I knew I wanted to be an announcer, so I did some research. When I found out a college degree wasn't required, I decided not to go." Even after so many decades in the field, Brianna still does not have a college degree.

Mobile and concert DJs also do not need a college degree. A technical degree or a music degree might help a DJ, but it is not required. "Some jobs will not hire you without a degree," Brianna says, "but being a DJ is a bit different. As long as you can perform the job well, people don't care what sort of education you have."

Wise Words

"To accomplish great things we must not only act, but also dream; not only plan, but also believe."
Anatole France

"Commit yourself to your own success and follow the steps required to achieve it."
Steve Maraboli

"Our work is to discover our work and then with all our heart to give ourselves to it."
—Buddha

If you would like to pursue a career as a DJ, the choice of whether or not to go to college is entirely up to you. There are benefits to attending, such as the opportunity to learn about music, journalism, or technology from an experienced teacher, but there are also reasons not to go. One disadvantage to attending college is the amount of money it costs. By the time a student graduates, he may owe tens of thousands of dollars.

Going to college full time might also prevent you from getting started on your career. Buying and learning how to use a DJ's equipment takes time, money, and practice. Some aspiring DJs decide not to go to college in order to get a head start on their careers.

Whether or not you choose to go to college or to become a DJ, take time to think about what your skills are and what makes you happiest. According to Brianna, "Nothing is more important than working at a job you love."

Find Out More

IN BOOKS

Brewster, Bill, and Frank Broughton. *Last Night a DJ Saved My Life: The History of the Disc Jockey*. New York: Grove, 2000.

Broughton, Frank, and Bill Brewster. *How to DJ Right: The Art and Science of Playing Records*. New York: Grove, 2003.

Staff, Mike. *How to Become a Radio DJ: A Guide to Breaking and Entering*. Troy, Mich.: Happy Communications, 1998.

ON THE INTERNET

Digital DJ Tips
www.digitaldjtips.com

DJ Master Course, "How Hard Is It to Become a DJ?"
blog.djmastercourse.com/how-hard-is-it-to-become-a-dj

U.S. Bureau of Labor Statistics, "Disc Jockey"
www.bls.gov/k12/music04.htm

Bibliography

DJ Master Course. "5 Tips on What Makes a Good DJ." http://blog.djmastercourse.com/5-tips-on-what-makes-a-good-dj (accessed March 20).

DJ To Hire. "How to Be a Mobile DJ." http://djtohire.hubpages.com/hub/How-to-Become-a-Mobile-DJ (accessed March 20).

eHow. "How Much Does a Mobile DJ Make?" http://www.ehow.com/info_8598820_much-mobile-dj-make.html (accessed March 20).

U.S. Bureau of Labor Statistics. "Occupational Outlook Handbook: Announcers." http://www.bls.gov/ooh/media-and-communication/announcers.htm (accessed March 20).

Wisegeek. "How Can I Become a Radio DJ?" http://www.wisegeek.org/how-can-i-become-a-radio-dj.htm (accessed March 20).

Index

About the Author

Christie Marlowe lives in Binghamton, New York, where she works as a writer and web designer. She has a degree in literature, cares strongly about the environment, and spends three or more nights a week wailing on her Telecaster.

Picture Credits